Sensing Light and Sound

by Jennifer Boothroyd

Lerner Publications Company · Minneapolis

LERNER

SOURCE

Expand learning beyond the printed book. Download free, complementary educational resources for this book from our website, www.lerneresource.com.

The images in this book are used with the permission of: © Goodshoot/Thinkstock, p. 4; © moodboard/Thinkstock, p. 5; © Purestock/Thinkstock, p. 6; © Katye Anderson/iStock/Thinkstock, p. 7; © Beatrix Boros/iStock/Thinkstock, p. 8; © iStockphoto.com/mashab_7ya, p. 9; © Allsorts Stock Photo/Alamy, p. 10; © iStockphoto.com/Serega, p. 11; © MIXA next/Thinkstock, p. 12; © iStockphoto.com/Paul Tessier, p. 13; © Jupterimages/Photos.com/Thinkstock, p. 14; © iStockphoto.com/YvanDube, p. 15; © iStockphoto.com/craftvision, p. 16; © iStockphoto.com/haveblue, p. 17; © iStockphoto.com/YanC, p. 18; © Joshua David Treisner/Shutterstock.com, p. 19; © iStockphoto.com/xubingruo, p. 20; © Noam Armonn/Hemera/Thinkstock, p. 21, © iStockphoto.com/CEFutcher, p. 22.

Front Cover: © Radius/SuperStock

Main body text set in ITC Avant Garde Gothic Std Medium 21/25.
Typeface provided by Adobe Systems.

Lerner Publications Company
A division of Lerner Publishing Group, Inc.
241 First Avenue North
Minneapolis, MN 55401 USA

For reading levels and more information, look up this title at www.lernerbooks.com.

Library of Congress Cataloging-in-Publication Data

Cataloging-in-Publication Data for *Sensing Light and Sound* is on file at the Library of Congress.
ISBN: 978–1–4677–3915–3 (LB)
ISBN: 978–1–4677–4688–5 (EB)

Manufactured in the United States of America
1 – CG – 7/15/14

Table of Contents

Your Senses   4

Seeing Light   7

Hearing Sound   12

Feeling Light and Sound   18

Glossary   23

Index   24

Your Senses

Your **senses** help you learn about the world.

Parts of your body **sense** things around you.

Sight, hearing, and touch
are a few of your senses.

Your eyes help you sense light.

Light enters your eyes. Your
brain tells you what you
are seeing.

Sunglasses shade your eyes.

Light can be too bright.

It is hard to see in the dark.

Light can be too **dim**.

Look around. What light
can you see?

Hearing Sound

Your ears help you sense sound.

You can't see sound vibrations.

Sound **vibrations** enter your ears.

Your brain tells you what
you are hearing.

Special gear protects this worker's ears.

Sound can be too loud.

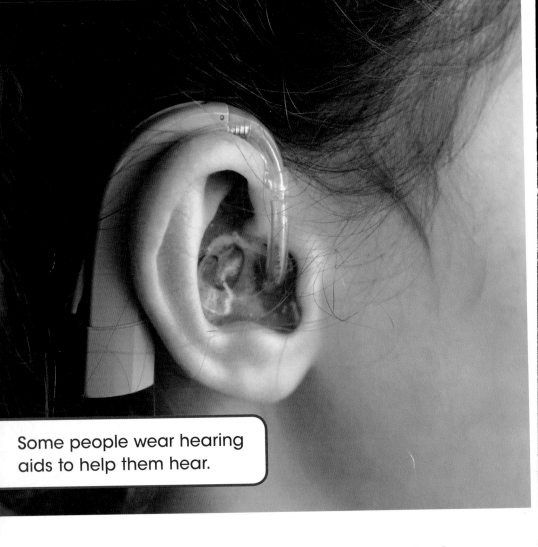

Some people wear hearing aids to help them hear.

Sound can be too quiet.

Listen.   What do you hear?

Feeling Light and Sound

Water ripples when sounds are loud.

You can sense sound without your ears.

You can feel sound vibrations.

Feel the sun on your face.

Sometimes you can sense
light without your eyes.

Many lights give off heat.
You can feel their warmth.

Find light and sound around you!

Glossary

dim – giving off very little light

sense – to gather information by feeling, hearing, seeing, tasting, and touching

senses – the ways your body gathers information about the world

vibrations – quick back-and-forth or side-to-side movements

Index

brain – 8, 14

bright – 9

dim – 10

ears – 12–13, 18

eyes – 7–8, 20

feel – 19–21

vibrations – 13, 19